EXPLORING ANGER

An Enchanté
Inner-Active Book

Written by the Enchanted Family
Illustrated by Tina Cash

Enchanté Publishing
120 Hawthorne, Palo Alto, CA 94301
1-800-473-2363

Concept by Ayman Sawaf, Liz Farrington, and Gudrun Höy. Design and art direction by Jaclyne Scardova.
 Printed in the U.S.A.
ISBN 1-56844-051-0

Foreword

The ability to feel is one of a child's most precious gifts. Every child is born with a deep desire to love and be loved. Underneath a child's anger, hurt, jealousy, and fear is love and a need to feel close. The people for whom children can sometimes feel the most negative emotion—parent, stepparent, sibling, teacher, friend—are those they also care most about. When it comes to feelings, no one is wrong.

Setting the stage for your child to be able to do this workbook, with optimal results, requires providing a place where the child can feel safe and have the necessary tools available for coloring and cutting. The book has been created so the child can do as much as possible on his/her own. However, you can assist by reading instructions, answering questions, and listening if your child wants to share. The Inner-Active workbooks are a unique and practical gift for children and all those who love and nurture them.

—Sirah Vettese, Ph.D., co-author of
Lifemates: The Love Fitness Program for a Lasting Relationship
—Harold H. Bloomfield, M.D., author of the best-selling
How to Survive the Loss of A Love and *How to Heal Depression*

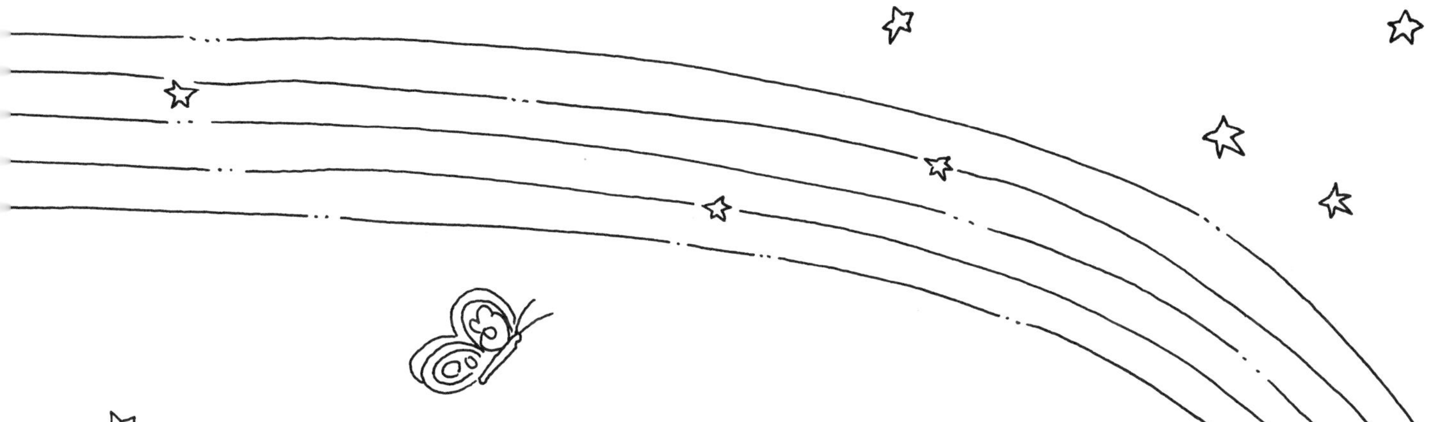

Introduction

Our most active emotion, anger is now being perceived as a primary root cause of most of today's personal, world, and physical maladies. Not anger itself, but unacknowledged anger, held in through repression or suppression, can be the emotional culprit underlying heart disease, cancer, marital and family disintegration, and most problems plaguing the world our children now enter. Anger arises from a violation of what each of us thinks "should" or "should not" happen. It is a real emotion, part of us as human beings, which can only be directed and channeled, not destroyed. Long misunderstood and feared, anger *can* be managed so we are freed of its potentially devastating effects.

Parents can help their children learn to process angry feelings from a very early age, allowing them to become forgiving individuals, unharmed by the anger which merely "passes through." As part of Enchanté's Emotional Literacy™ campaign, this book encourages your child to release anger and translate its energy into beauty and enthusiasm.

—Ilene L. Dillon, M.S.W.,
author of *Exploring Anger With Your Child*

What color is anger to you?
Draw a picture of something using
the color you think of when you are angry.

What do you think anger looks like?

Draw a picture or design showing how anger looks to you.

How do you look when you are angry?
Draw a picture in the frame of what you might look like when you are angry.

ANGRY

Write or draw the answers to the questions below.

What makes you angry?

How do others know when you are angry?

How do grown-ups act when they are angry?

How do you know when others are angry at you?

Scribble angrily using any colors.
On a separate sheet of paper, scribble another angry picture. When you have finished, tear it into as many pieces as you can.

Listed below are ways to deal with your angry feelings. Make a check under "OKAY" or "NOT OKAY" for each one.

	OKAY	**NOT OKAY**
Punch a pillow	________	________
Slam doors	________	________
Yell at someone	________	________
Work in the garden	________	________
Talk things over	________	________
Beat someone up	________	________
Stamp my feet	________	________
Binge on food	________	________
Rip up old newspapers	________	________
Bounce a ball	________	________
Play with clay	________	________
Jump on the bed	________	________
Run and scream outside	________	________
Throw a temper tantrum	________	________
Hurt myself	________	________
Be mean to the pet	________	________

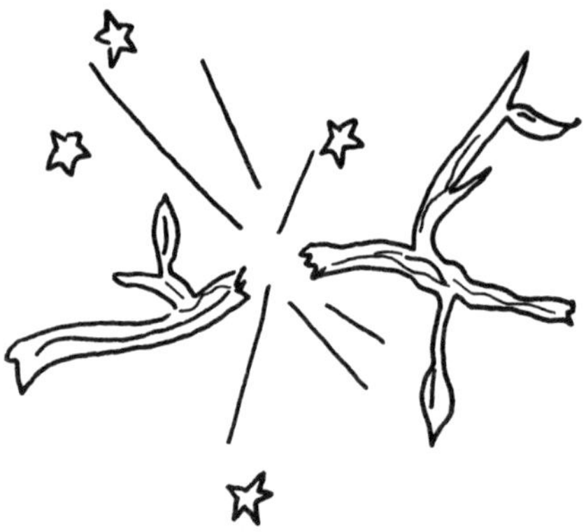

Write down other good ways to deal with your anger:

Complete the following sentences with your own feelings.

I am most angry about... ______________________________

____

I feel angry when my dad/stepdad... ___________________

____

I feel angry when my mom/stepmom... __________________

____

I feel angry when my brother or sister... ______________

____

I feel angry when my friend... _________________________

____

I feel angry when my teacher...________________________

____

Make a badge that you can color and wear
to let others know that you feel angry.
You can also make a sign for the door.

~WARNING~
I'M MAD
ONE
ANGRY
PERSON
ANGRY
STAY BACK

Write a letter to the person who has made you angry. Tell the person what he or she said or did that made you angry — and why. This is your private letter.

Color the picture as you follow the path.

1. Imagine you are walking on the mountain path and you are very angry.
2. You have been walking and walking, feeling angry for a long time.
3. Is there any way you can let go of your anger?
4. You hear the rushing of water.
5. As you turn the corner, you see a sparkling waterfall.

6. Standing next to the waterfall, you see a beautiful rainbow.
7. You walk into the pool of clear water.
8. You swim over to the waterfall. Stand quietly and let the magic water wash away all your angry feelings.
9. Step out of the water, calm and peaceful.
10. Reach out and wrap yourself in a rainbow.

Now that you know the path to the magic waterfall, close your eyes and imagine yourself going to that place of peace and quiet where anger melts away.

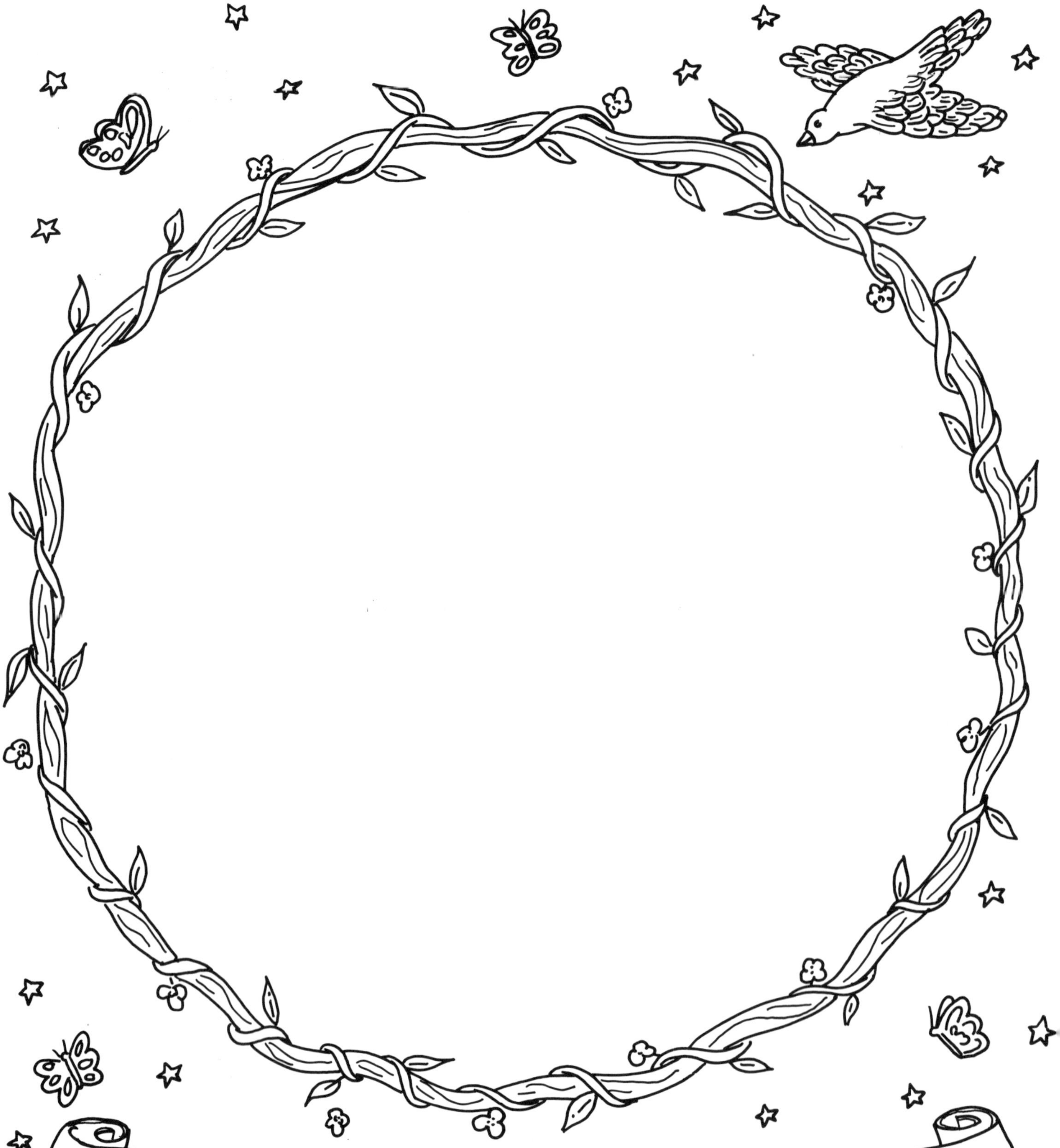

In the center of the circle, draw a picture
of yourself when you are not angry.

Anger is an energy. Let it out, but not onto someone else.
It is hurtful when you keep it inside or express
it in ways that hurt others.